Mortal, Everlasting

Mortal, Everlasting

Jeffrey Levine

Pavement Saw Press
Columbus, Ohio

ACKNOWLEDGEMENTS

The Alembic, The Antioch Review, The Beloit Poetry Journal, Barrow Street, Cimarron Review, Crab Orchard Review, The Emily Dickinson Award Anthology, 5 AM, ForPoetry.com, GSU Review, Hayden's Ferry Review, The Kerf, Kestrel, Luna, Many Mountains Moving, Mississippi Review, Missouri Review, Nimrod, North American Review, Notre Dame Review, Poetry International, Ploughshares, Quarter After Eight, Quarterly West, Virginia Quarterly Review, Yankee Magazine. *Dawn With Cardinals,* and *One Month Before His 50th Birthday,* were republished on Poetry Daily (www.poems.com). *Dawn, With Cardinals, One Month Before His 50th Birthday, Penelope Draws From Life, Telemachus in San Miguel,* and *Turns Out Circe Has Something of a Past* were awarded the 1999 Larry Levis Award by the editors of The Missouri Review.

Editor: David Baratier
Associate Editor: Stephen Mainard
Cover Photograph: Jeffrey Levine
Cover and book design by William Kuch, WK Graphic Design

Printed in Canada

Pavement Saw Press
PO Box 6291
Columbus, OH 43206
pavementsaw.org

Products are available through the publisher or through:
SPD, 1341 Seventh St., Berkeley, CA 94710 • 800.869.7553

Winner of the 2000 Transcontinental Poetry Award for an outstanding first book-length collection of poetry or prose.
We read yearly from June 1st until August 15th.
Send an SASE for information.

Pavement Saw Press is a not for profit corporation, any donations are greatly appreciated and are considered charitable tax donations under section 501(c) of the federal tax code.
Paper Trade: ISBN 1-886350-73-6
Cloth Cover: ISBN 1-886350-74-4

Contents

One

Two

Three

I had as lief be embraced by the porter at the hotel
As to get no more from the moonlight
Than your moist hand.

Be the voice of night and Florida in my ear.
Use dusky words and dusky images.
Darken your speech.

Wallace Stevens, *Two Figures in Dense Violet Light*

In memory of Bernie Friedland.
Mortal, Everlasting

ONE

Blisses

After leaving even then you promised to return
each week, water the plants, unhinge my armor
then lay it out piece by blighted piece
and in my borrowed skin, bathe what remained of me.

After leaving even then you promised—as a vow—
made in gesture folding in upon itself like paper—
to honor our slow voices, and the sun beneath
the small mountain where it rests even now

as a drop of water, a low bell, a scrap of wind torn free
from a night of vows. Now, with your gesture you would
have kept this sacrament, and even then your mouth took
a shape only I could see, quivered, mute.

But I could see, and though in truth you said so little
maybe this is only something I thought composed
the foreground —fruit mounded in your hands—
like blisses: everlasting, pungent, crackling, gone.

Asphodel

Flower, array of fertile and sterile leaves,
"forming the reproductive fabric of angiosperms,"
my friend, the botanist, says,

a tube inserted in her chest below the breast,
through a cleft and fixed to a pump
she calls Marion, after her doctor.

Marion doses her chemo, day and night—her stem,
tendril, style—the elongated unfertile portion of the pistil,
she explains, between the stigma and ovulary, her fruit.

She's wildflower—pipewort, or carrion wort,
depending—false Solomon's seal,
nodding mandarin, asphodel.

Ziggurat of marzipan? she asks,
producing delicate smoked salmon,
lifting a gold-plated butterfish to my mouth.

When it rains, she says in a soft, clear voice,
the waters come so hard, the desert earth
cannot absorb. Torrential. Useless.

Her pose is a diagram of gesture—weight forward
on left leg, right behind, toe brushing floor
in decorous point, palms open, turned front.

She's learning a little Arabic from a phrase book:
"Uncle, may I take an apple and an orange?"
"Of course, help yourself, son; we have peaches, too."

"Barbara, taste how sweet this peach is."
(Taste the peach this, of Barbara, see tasty how.)
*Yálla (*come on)

Let's cut a melon; they are very sweet.
íhna imbasát-na hína
(We enjoyed it here.)

Elegy in Istanbul

What's given up amazes everyone,
as the wonder of what remains—pink and tender—

each body celebrates its losses, body leaving body,
arcing out in dimmed rhythm like the seer

who rubs your shoulders hard enough
to press out virgin oil, and later others wash

the towels until the last traces vanish from the nap—
linens shelved into one long ballet blanc.

Two smocked women in a narrow room strip
layers from an antique canvas—

scuff through to faintest pentimento,
a master's oils alloyed in a crucible of berries, roots.

So meticulously they work, they start to love their hands,
love each layer as it flowers beneath their hands.

The layers flake to dust, settle like hoarfrost
to the pitted floor.

At day's end, flecked smocks pegged, the linings warm
and worn, abalone buttons fracture

under jaded fingers like dime-store paint, half-
Caravaggio, half-mystic, these artisans,

their patience out of nothing, but somewhere
something solid lives. As there,

through the half-light of dusk, someone's returning berries
to the berry bush, replacing each just so,

and in winter, too.

Plum Trees

We lay flank to flank, my brother and I,
brushed by the thinning blood, its russet warmth.
"Don't be cross," he asked.

Or my mother asked.
Over the phone, kitchen window,
cardinal-watching, her three vermilion families.
I know this though we're talking long distance.
I've put in my time at that window.

She wanted to ask about her other son,
but stopped, imprisoned star, caught in the instant's freezing.
If he appears in fire, a thousand lights contend for him
mid a vault of thorns.

La volta degli spini, I offered.
"What?"
Shredded, trampled, furrowed night.

"Oh. The smoke always smells so bitter.
Why is that, dear?"

Every so often she happens on a soap
that reminds her of the children
when they were babies.

"I wish he would talk to me," she whispered.
I told her my nine-year-old can distinguish
eight different species of pigeon in the city:
Pied-Splash, Blue-Bar, Checker, Red—

A good eye identifies 28 color morphs,
or feather patterns, I told my mother, who
was not listening. She wanted to know
when the next lunar eclipse would come.

You must learn to measure time precisely,
to plot the angle through the eyes—
opposite over hypotenuse, I reminded her.
Let x = sine. She began to sob.

"What of the doves? Tell me more."
Chaste and faithful, *columbina simplicitas*—simple.
Be ye wise as serpents and harmless as doves, says the Bible.
Though they flee, tremble, in terror of the eagle, the hawk.

"Why only to you?"
The cardinals eat and drink ceaselessly and well.
She says they are "delighted" and too tremulous to sing.

Optics deceive. Music lies.
Their geometry encourages unjust dominion
and mathematics, avarice.

The sun falls in tufts of cotton from its place in the heavens.
Oh, you night of grasses, she said.
She had forgotten her quotes.

I ask only the barefoot light on the sleeping land.
I need to think of a proof for her.
An oracle with cold lips and vaporous thought.
Even a single blade of tasseled wheat.
My brother's skin at seven years, saffron
toasted in the sun, doe-eyed, a wounded bird.

Each night, his house turns to stone,
too cold for you, I warned my mother.
Our bodies cover themselves with vines of syllables.
Our murmurs collect in pitchers on the terrace.

She pours them over the roots of the old
and gnarled plum trees—
just before they flower, just before they fruit.

Am, Therefore

old pond
frog jumps in
plop
—Basho

We noticed a towering tree trading compound leaves
for a mutiny of yellow blooms. *Cassia fistula.*
You like the sound of that?

Monstera deliciosa. Delicious Monster.
You can eat the spike coming out of the bloom.
Milk and Wine Lily. Lobster Claw. Firebrush.
Woman's Tongue. Jerusalem Thorn.
Look here. Pelican Flower.
Feel how nice the leaves lay.

The unopened flowers shaped themselves like pelicans,
a pointed beaked crest arched
into two wide wings folded down in rest.

I picked the largest flower, webbed it in my hands.
It seemed an egg, ready to give birth to a small life.

My son studied the blossom as if he might find a flaw,
tossed it to the ground.

This plant's good for shade, comes from Africa.
This one here will kill you.
This one's best for keeping dirt on hillsides.
Some eat and smoke these seeds to feel nice.

The guide pulled the milky green buds from the ylang-ylang,
squeezed them between his red fingertips
so my son could taste the essence.

This tree was brought here by Captain Bligh,
you know, of the Bounty.
Now everybody's eating breadfruit, even the hogs.
Everybody still praying to the Captain.

Oh come back, Master Bligh, come back.
Bring me a woman, bring me a husband,
bring me a pot to cook in,
bring me a piece of meat to eat with this breadfruit.

I will be the perfect swimmer, the guide said,
staring at my little boy, free
of the air and the boundaries of the living,
down, down, to kiss the silt of the ocean floor,
touch the bottom of the world with numb fingers.

My son shrugged, that way he has.

Below the treetops, the ocean turned its back,
glistened, canescent with glare,
waves struggling in and out, leaving
their small carnations of foam.

My Mother's Spine

I'm searching on the Amtrak for Ulysses' name in Greek,
thinking, this is crazy, I know this word, can see his men
turned to swine, when Oedipus boards in Baltimore

with Clytemnestra and Orestes at his heels, and look!
when we stop in Philly there's my Uncle Jack, his mouth mottled
with challah crumbs, so the car is filling up with mortals too,

and still that name gone to powder like petals pressed and blown
away, left only bare stems curved like Ulysses' bow
just before he finished off his wife's suitors, and now

here's Dawn, not the rosy-fingered thing, a long-ago lover
who spoke a little Russian, played the wine-dark cello—
that I can remember—and the day my mother called us home,

my brother in the bathtub, blood so deep, deep red,
blackened to the bottom, my mother sculpting his face
in her hands, and me shaking and shaking him

10 as red fell through and through our arms, water falling
in small red rivers to the floor. Walking later, windy, bitter cold,
Dawn wouldn't let me kiss her, even though he survived,

the jazz pianist with a gift for the half-diminished chord,
who calls now and then so I'll know he's alive. But the name
is coming, I can feel Ulysses' bow bent near breaking,

bent like my mother's spine, which has softened and so
needs to ossify, the doctor says, though to me the word sounds
less of harden, more an exotic shore bird, say,

with radiant plumage and a pliant, gently curving neck—
a bird that wants the early light for the way everything brightens
to a kind of pink—shell pink—color you see behind

the florist's case, daybunch roses no one ever buys,
fragile and short lived, because the idea wears
into the word and the word into one of those whelks

or scallop shells you find above the tide line—scrubbed
so smooth the sky might move clear through them.
Tossed back, they dissolve into metals and salt

as they fall below the breakers, alien somehow,
sick for home, like Odysseus himself—and thank God!
Here he is at last—in beggar's clothes and blood-soaked rags,

black ship moored, his spine old and bent the way
my mother's arced away from me when I tried to hug her
on my brother's ward, swayed back toward his bed.

Row of Blue Flowers

I gave a final look, awoke in Prague speaking a language
made of cakes and stew. Chilly. You wear warm things in Prague,
even without a body. Though you're light, so light without it.

My spirit in its bed motioned with the slightest breath,
its hair spread against the pillow. I entered its eyes
as a plane flies into a vast cloud and sees no other realm.

I told it something. Maybe how we suffer for our preferences,
that this life not be like one thing or another. It admitted me
as light of a certain density, and I filled its breathing.

I swam its nakedness from the inside, commandeered its neck
with the troops at my charge, this mouth, shoulders, chest.
I shuddered with its shudder. I did not ask how my spirit came

to be in Prague. Day after day I collected in eddies, spun heart
with its own blue thread. If it spoke to me, I heard only the sound
of rogue waves, the pitch and roll of open sea.

The dream it woke me from indulged fire, lanterns, embers, heat.
My spirit pleaded to return to my body in the snow.
I offered instead Istanbul, a feast of *pirinc corba, beyendeli kebap.*

I offered *mahia,* alcohol distilled from fruit,
a long drought on my *sebsi,* a morning at *souk,*
trancing of *tbola,* the side drum played with sticks.

There's a cut of land, the bleached, swath of wind,
shadows crossing a snowy lawn where what was me still lay
all late afternoon, blue with cold.

I know what rolled my body over in the snow,
fed me back my soul. I tried to say it. Lost in itself.
The doctor asked what day it was, what year, what time.

It must have been morning—light at the window.
Do you mean time to which the heart surrenders?
I asked her, while she held my wrist, admitted there's no cure,

no out-of-the-cirrus intervention. Look, I've done
what I wanted to do. Suppose this cell-by-cell dissolve segues
into a bud-by-bud renewal—all dibber, loam and trowel.

I passed by me this evening, an impression in the snow.
There's my face in profile: two arms, two legs,
what must have been my chin. It's said

the age of the fishes and loaves is done
and day is an irksome thing and full of glare.
An yet. Something saved me, some tuneful piping.

With such clarity I plant the row of blue flowers,
make new plans for electricity in the house,
my heart growing wider and wider.

My compliments to the fishes.
My compliments to the loaves.
My compliments to the snow, deep and soft.

Finger Painting

In the corner of my study, a yellow sun,
my own boy's brightest yet, whistling in the pigment,
ringing through the center, out beyond the edges
and onto his shirt and cuffs with its blinding arms,
its god-giving light,

and I start daubing it myself,
five wet fingers in the cool, wet paints—
my fingers twist the shapes of crooked streets,
slurring thumbs through the pigment-ooze—

dark figures melt into whitewashed tavernas
where heart-throbs sing generic love songs, the ones
you hear in Venice or Madrid, or heard once
when travel happened slowly, and you held back
the curtained windows as music lifted
off the cobblestones and cool palms pressed
your shoulders, a low front gathering off the coast.

The art paper stiffens under paint. That smell—
oil, vanilla, nail polish, ice? Last time
I sat here dazed, the maple outside burned
bright enough to blind me, and sugar sap ran
black and wet through the bark
where a ten-penny nail pinned the sparrow feeder
to the tree and it took me, my wife said, all day
to hear her knocking at the door.

Picasso's Pantaloons

Last time out for stone crabs, my grandfather pointed
to the hotel he chose for Selma when she was his girl,
his ancient finger warped a light year gone,
faint trail of dust between his chair and the Milky Way,

so I thought love is like a bluebottle fly, not
the fly itself, but the color, which is not blue but bottle-green,
the color of my son's eyes, and makes the same sounds,
the heart, not the fly—sound of a key in the lock,
sound of the sky gone pink,
a sky that wants to give away its coins.

After, when there's nothing overhead but a thread of coral,
a brief calm holds its breath above the bay.
Wind comes later—first a caress, then the pawing—
and you're safe as Picasso's last model
when the Maestro struts his drawstring pantaloons
and something climbs the studio like a liana toward the light.

Walking the apartment room to room—
bed sheets taut as a Navy cot, tins of crab meat stacked
upon the shelves, ice evaporated from the metal tray— *15*
just that white apron of ice—my little boy says,
"Yep, Great Grandpa's dead all right."

My own father, in his seventies, alive,
running down through Spain, sends me postcards
from Madrid with Picasso's colors, Picasso's face, his words—

Vivir, to live, *Amor*—haven't we always known that one?
How children learn to parrot love,
how the shadows linger in the eaves when you kill the lights.

Some days, for practice, I think of my father already dead—
another empty room, my brothers,
one fly humming at the window—
how my son looks at me, looks down.

This is what I imagine sometimes
for practice,
how my son studies the ground.

The blue planet recedes below, and I see its curve within

the evidence of cultivated grains,
sea grasses, the single transcendent thing
signaling return from the colorless world:
flame of red poppy in the garden,
you in your yellow pajamas, growing
smaller and smaller until nothing's left
but yellow cloth and smooth pearl buttons.

And a long slow stillness between takes.
Long enough to go glib with the glossary of cinema,
its nest of word-blind words:
jump cut, metaphorical dissolve, crosscut shot.

One settles for optical effect, transition.
The superimposed disappearance of one scene
and appearance of the next.

The cinematographer has a mind of her own.
Range and angle. Frame.
She becomes the softgrowth inside the heart,
the snowbed underneath us all.

Out of range, out of script, survivors carry water,
they carry food, from one place to the next.

Put another way, happiness is transitional,
fruit of restlessness, the thoughtful pose.

Apparently there is no difference
between one world and the next.
Same deep dish filled with yearning,
same days trellised, where we climb as best we can.
One world a little closer, one a bit more distant.

Have a glass of Zinfandel, have it anyway,
ruby colored, feral and ruby,
run hot water in the tub.

Let's wash our hair together in the snowbed
under this intricate canopy, this overhanging firmament,
this magical roof fretted, quick before it goes.

What We Don't Speak About

Not the house deep under trees that hold
off the heat, or who will take the room
with gardens on two sides, the room alone.

Of the finches, yes,
but not the single Monarch, how she drinks
for three days, crazy with desire
before letting the wind carry her
to Mexico or Tanzania.

And never, not once, of the purple-crested lourie,
creaking its cry that says "Africa"
and means "servant." How much
of our home is an abandoned chunk of earth,
or how like the continents we drift on fields
of heather—to lay down in it—wanting that too.

In the old days we'd point:
"See what we've carved out of the trees, the grasslands.
See the house, it could be ours,
the animals, the plants, the good strong roof."
Knowing neither of us saw.
Not the guava which belonged to the cook,
in tears, blaming us for unkind hearts—
her guava, hers.

Without warning, souls detach:
not that surely, neither how we might forget it all,
nor how October hangs over the land
and with a word, falls apart, remembers
nothing of itself. Or a bit more wind
and the lanterns fail.

The Misunderstanders

What the Lord keeps secret is no
concern of yours.
—Ecclesiastes 3:21

Somewhere in the Babylonian Talmud it is written,
God kissed Moses on the mouth.
I can't find it in my Bible, not anywhere—
though they spend a long, long time together alone
upon the mountaintop, God and Moses,

so it must be there, locked inside the ink,
locked inside the obedient and trembling hand
that held the pen, before the hand turned to stone
and the kiss to stone and the stone kept its counsel.

There's the face of God, his arm and fingers, mouth—
but when it came to breathing life into Adam
the Lord sent an angel, a second,
who must have liked it here among us
or liked the kissing too,
because he drew back ten thousand more—
angels who surround us in our beds and at our tables—
the front seats our cars,
but have trouble with our language.

Male bodies they have, says the Talmud,
indistinguishable from God himself,
but for the wings, or do I just imagine wings
the way I see our passions having wings?

These messengers, then, take orders,
make deliveries: breath of life, kiss of death,
and always overhearing but not getting what we say.

Better not to understand,
and better still, raise misunderstanding to an art.
There's an ironic God for you—a God worth knowing.

A rueful God—

I will blot out from the earth the men whom I created—
Men together with the beasts,
creeping things, and birds of the sky;
For I regret that I made them.

Does his love for Moses turn to stone?
"One kiss may ruin a human life."
I forget who said it.

Some presume when God turned his back
he only meant to hide his genitals,
turn away and fasten up his robe.

God has genitals?
So then the angels.

Still, God trusts none of them,
none of us.

Who's more guarded than this God of ours,
20 blessed be he, keeper of secrets,
who sends his angels to watch us in our daily lives,
and causes them to misunderstand?

Liturgy

> If there must be a god in the house…
> Let him move as sunlight moves on the floor
> — *Wallace Stevens*

All this year our weather happened indoors.
All light, borrowed light.

The lake, the predawn glow of cabins on the shore,
an anchor lamp, the incandescent moon.
All burned a taller, darker twin on water.

Endless, our gift for complicating simplest things.

A breeze lifts the curtain of an open window.
From some other room, bright, crystalline bars,
and then low bars of a piano, some old air.

Slight acrid scent, astringent polish, rubbing alcohol.

I enter the small chapel at San Juan Capistrano
where Junípero Serra celebrated mass,
kneel to say a prayer for my brother,
a prayer that pleads like a scalpel, or should,
but a camera flashes at the rear.

Tourists examine the crucifix; one laughs.
They come to feed the birds.
This day I make for the sun-stippled cloister.

Confluence of earth, cut of land, or its fold,
bleaching sky, swath of wind, length
of shadows. One has only to love
what ripens: Yesterday,

the sweet corn wasn't ready,
tomorrow will be too late.
Light the fire beneath the pot.

Andes

Quito perches mid-planet, mid-cloud,
higher peaks rising up and up,
east and west, like green imperial armies,
walling the city on both flanks—
volcanic bird, her feet dusted with ash.

She breathes the inconsequence sea level,
the distant inconsequence of sea,
and speaks a language swimming
in too thin air, too thick with idioms—
a tongue that loves its vowels, worships consonants—
her counterpoint, dashing and languid,
stocky, mustachioed and suave.

I think you'd like this city.
I think it would appeal to some part of you that wants—
I don't know—wants.

Presumptuous of me, yes, but listen:
twenty multi-colored flags, flutes and condors,
and the sky parched blue-gray and mutable.
Clouds slide overhead like fresh lava—
equatorial brilliance cooling to burnt toast
and back again, the light changing by moments,
and changing the moments themselves
into more than themselves—
that sort of want—
the kind that lasts and outlasts.

You'd melt at the exchange rate of illumination—
merest gossamer to blinding incandescence,
mild yellows, greens, indigo, violet—
then fields of glint, glare, glow seizing
the white colonial facades,
buffing the tile-domed churches
and iron statues, polishing

the Winged Madonna on the mount,
her face awash in luster and lava, wanting
everything at once for us,
wanting for nothing at all.

Man Washing the Floor at Daybreak, the Lodgers Out

A hummingbird thrums the windowpane
scattering light over the adobe, through the spruce.

Drawing his mop over the Spanish tiles,
the ropes loosen and quiver like horses' flanks

while side-by-side impressions linger in the lodgers' pillow
and lank embers hiss fire in the old language.

He wants to leave their breakfast untouched on the table
where ants busy themselves erasing every trace.

Once a seer, an *adivina,* said, it's himself he visits
pace by pace, the untouched part, those *his* angels

he's cursed into being year by year, tile by tile,
these past nights gathered in his one good ear.

He imagines harvests ripening to gold, the lodger's passing
while the sun rivers the shapes of iron pipes,

the day's plumbing gone umber with rust, in the earthen bowl
the mango striped and turned to stone.

Glazunov's Azaleas

They remind him from a distance of the melon colored light
above the Rivers of Babylon, and closer, of Li Po—

"On Hearing The Flute At Lo-Cheng One Spring Night,"
for example, or "On the Ship of Spicewood."

If only I'd postponed my birth, he thought, my texts would set
themselves as antiphons of true and tempered triads,

filled with tonal flux and vague scales torn
from my nights at the Blue Ox Lodge

where I learned my bitter melodies far
from this sweet smell that cuffs me,

and I regret those wasted Bacchanals—
what could I have been thinking, of all things?

Raymonda! Ballet! Dance!
Damn my impatience and Francophylian funk!

I spent my wad on Les Sylphides,
teaching M. Chopin how the pillar of flute might play,

how clarinets with their rose wood sing
in that register, so conspiratorial and low—

and me from St. Petersburg to Boulogne—
even Satan fell no farther. Oh forgive,

it's always the critics, those dark brothers,
who fail me: "warm, gracious, grand."

The flesh, as always, takes on the pure poise of spirit,
something about the kingfisher's cunning,

the lip of stone, the river moving, moving—
Now there's a libretto worth a farthing and a half—

with sprays for strings, wrist-thick cascades in ascending thirds,
brass piled high against the iron spiles, and oh, don't forget

the gypsy and her dreadful fear of stars.
So I carried my azaleas south, and further south.

Bowls of copal burned spirals at the café in Cholula
where they serve a drink called, "Blood of the Composer."

They always put a maraschino cherry in the cup.
They use it to mean the maestro's heart.

Mikhail Ivanovich Glinka at the Swim-Up Bar

Think of Van Gogh, needled by that ringing in his ear,
of Nijinsky in his straitjacket, of Robert Schumann.
Yes, think of Schumann, whose wedded bliss lasted
only four years before his mind betrayed him.
Not even Clara could save him from madness.
Not even she. If my wife were here, she'd say,

"Honey, don't forget Dianne Arbus or Plath."
And what about Virginia Woolf, contemplating
each stone she sewed into her sweater
before she waded into the stream.

Think of them all, I nod to myself,
though there must be other etcetera
to distill into palliatives, every plum
of suffering, every genus of indifference.

Even now, when I listen to my music
I catch myself muttering, "Fool."
Fool who made the sorrows of all souls count
as nothing even as I squeezed the crystal,
everything vanished into the umlauts of Berlin nights.
Even my scores lightened, rose as cloud.

These days, I no longer need to sleep.
I remember, have always remembered too much.
No matter. The Hermitage, that ridiculous little gusli,
the Bolshoi. Computer problems with the Mir.
Bach's Brandenburgs as played by six dozen balalaikas.
This is what they want to know about in the Provinces,
I tell Vladimir, the mixer at the swim-up bar,
the Four Seasons in Duesseldorf.

Vladimir looks as though he listens closely, I'll give him that,
those silver wings tucked tight behind him,
angelic concern spread behind his Cossack moustache,
right finger checking and rechecking
the geography of his saber scar for luck.

There's one conversation we've never had,
and Vlad leans into me, refills my Stoli on the house,
adds some ice—Say I loved Ludmila,
say how Ruslan comes to me speaking
one night with a voice made of cellos,
then next night keening like massed bassoons.

Say I even craved those nightly visitations—
that they awoke in me my Spanish dreams,
hummed a Jota Aragonesa, my Memory
of a Summer Night in Madrid,
though I've never been.

Oh, Vlad, you should have heard my dreams.
Like an eight-armed goddess retelling
the lives of czars while peeling oranges
and humming *Prince Igor* as I bowed.

Vincent's Auction

A little worn, but trim, Van Gogh watches the auction
from a folding chair in the back row.
In Christie's, nobody recognizes him.
He'd like to have the painting back, hang it
above the sofa in his Hoboken loft,
but there's just a handful of guilders
and two francs in his purse.

In his dream he saw her again.
Parched lawns overgrown with thistle.
Death had transformed her into a student
from a religious school, a pious girl
in a long-sleeved dress, which came down past her ankles.
Walking along a rusty irrigation pipe, he followed,
her back dissolved in silver haze.

At the wood's edge she stopped and turned,
forehead glowing in the moonlight.
A skeletal pallor covered her cheeks,
teeth gleaming, her eyes hidden
by the dark glasses of the blind,
she pointed with dry fingers at her brother,
"Look what they've done to you."

Through closed windows high above the auction,
the sound of a cello—
someone practicing a passage over and over.
If only he could change his material state,
become air, or stone, or crane.

Searching for a tablet and charcoal,
he studies the young woman on the dais,
the way she brings her hair forward
until it spreads over her dress, covers her left breast—
he follows her in his mind through streets and alleys,
gates and flights of steps, stone-paved courtyards.
He has no palette to stop her.
Nothing to stop himself.

It rained. Not hard. Not pouring.
A thick dampness in the air.
Van Gogh remembered the mailbox key
still lying on his desk.

Certain that God is not religious,
even so, while watching a sudden storm overtake
a wheat field flocked with crows,
he once saw the world created new.

In the morning, he'll open his shutters
on the beginning of a winter day—
a nameless feeling in the dove-colored light—
a contentment lighter than any in life.

TWO

Ulysses Hears the Spirit on the Stairs

That time I called my son from a hotel
in Hunan province, he wanted me to rub his back
the way I do most nights. Not knowing what to say,
we said nothing, only breathing, then, "Rub harder!"
but he couldn't feel my hands, just my breath
where the phone pressed against his ear.

Now I'm wakened by the sound of my own breathing.
In my dream, I've been talking to my lover's husband on the phone.
But when I try to will my eyes open the other man draws me back,
points out I'm the "other man," not he.

He volunteers his wife sleeps in another room,
sometimes sees her nightgown pass,
quick silk rustle and long exhale,
"There, not there," he says,
like one of those enormous moths you find by moonlight,
luminescent, glowing green or blue, around its fleeting life.

He describes the outline of her breasts, and I'm confused,
do moths have breasts, isn't it wings they have?
But it's my lover he's trying to unlearn, and already
I regret we'll have no more talks like this.

His son can only shrug when no one speaks at dinner.
I say mine likes the aquarium for the jellyfish—
not things so much as souls afloat
in their faintly phosphored otherness, down or up,
which way seeming not to matter to them, or us.
It's like watching something vague move without a body, gently,
so not to bruise.

There's nothing else to say,
so we fix instead on something more exact—
a blaze of parrot tulips beneath the sugar maple,
the taste of a perfect orange sectioned on a Chinese tray,
or the sound of small boys breathing in their cocoons—
until we can breathe the morning too,
hair slicked back, door open.

One month before his 50th birthday,

Ulysses took up weighing himself after sex.
Hair wet, arms sore, still he felt it urgent as sleep
after months of sailing or a month of wine,
when home sounded a faint, remembered song,
the men's silk tents engorged with treasure and willing slaves
cordoned a bruised & blooded coast.

Penelope could hear him open the walk-in closet
where he kept the bathroom scale,
springs move, balance shift.

If the sex was good, she'd be talking about something,
I don't know—
their cliff-top house, what needed doing.
About their son, surly & distant, who seemed to disapprove of her.

He might have set a better example for the boy, Ulysses guessed,
but wouldn't say—obvious,
& besides, he'd be in the walk-in weighing himself,
then shower & not think about it anymore—
weight or sons, foreign treasure.

He'd climb into bed again,
pick up an old crossword puzzle while Penelope
hooked a robe over her shoulder,
crooked her finger through the loop the way his sailors
cozied their pea coats in port towns,
streets whitened, bleached,

and Ulysses would watch Penelope cross the room,
bracelets coppered around her wrists,
her face red from sex, still striking in some lights—
this light, morning light—then look away—
so she wouldn't catch him marking the beauty spots
on her left breast, her shoulders, rump.

Below, a black ship laded butts of salted meat
while his wife made the faucet squeak
and steam slipped beneath the bathroom door.

Dawn, With Cardinals

After separating from Penelope, Ulysses
takes a smallish cottage out of town,
bounded by deep woods on one side, a golf course on the other
where children sled or startle frogs, depending on the season.

Crows strut their turf under plum trees, furl their capes
and bob like drunks. Of the night birds, owls map the taller pines
with iridescent eyes, and moon hens peck at drops of evening dew.

When the divorce is done, he'll move,
settle on a narrow road beside a spit of sand—beyond that, sea.
He could earn a modest pension crafting bird feeders from mill scraps,
keep a brace of hunting dogs for company,
rake the silt for clams and oysters at low tide.

For now, he contents himself recording bird calls,
but forgets them quickly as he learns, save
the cardinal's song,
a slight and mournful chirping
heard each morning just outside his porch.

And always the same two birds—
she quarrelsome,
he quiet or detached or maybe mystified
at his helplessness to make a difference.
Or cocksure he does—
you see it in the ebony beak, crimson breast. Look—

the bird bath's full of cool clear water and still
she carries on, sharp staccato chirps, high pitched, unwavering.
He flutters but makes no sound, something holding on
inside him, something faintly chipped.

Ulysses never planned to wake so early every morning.
Who believes in ritual for days or weeks, until it's a proven thing?
But here it is, persistent, regular.
Ulysses lets dawn filter through the screened porch.

First no light, then light.
First no birds,
then song.
No wind; wind.

Goddesses in the Vieux Carre

Summer falls thick as water, like the Balm of Sorrows
between the fingers, and it feels so cool and waxy
why resent the family in the magazine,
he drying dishes while watching the light unfold his wife's hair,
she leafing through the spring bulbs—
thumbs the early crocus, white and purple tulips,
the children all with the taste of pie in their mouths—

Ulysses checks into the Pontchartrain where waiters orbit
in satin vests, rotate on their heels like servile planets.
One removes the salad forks, another bears iced silver
in linen napkins, "Chilled forks for the salad," and of course
Ulysses laughs, the waiters, too—
at themselves, the silver, wet linen—
how the suffering are served.

The maitre d' dips his bony fingers into a basket
blossoming with plums,
he bites into two at once
while mumbling through the reservations, names lifted
from the Book of the Dead.

There's svelte Cybele at the next table,
an immortal worshiped by the Syrians.
Smart dresser, she tosses Ulysses a bright green apple
and bewitching smile.

By the bar, the baleful Goddess of Slit Poppies prepares
another kind of sacrifice.
And already in his back pocket,
someone's pager number, Kali, "Dark Mother of Time."

Women are all goddesses in the South, Ulysses knows—
and not at all like ones he's known before.
Look there, on the patio, the backs of deities in soft dresses
walking hand-in-hand through the spotted light—

Lady of the Serpent Skirts, the Mayan Moon Goddess drenched
in crinoline, and Penelope, his ex-wife,
now with untold powers of her own—

But Ulysses can't help loving every face he sees—
spell casters swayed to Zydeco, jeweled warriors
with their mirrored shields, and blue jeaned heralds of the harvest.
She who would restore his youth.
How choose?

Ulysses doesn't know the taste that brought him here
or whose idea first the eating was,
only that every apple was commanded,
each plum riper than the last,
and all the pies forbidden.

Shall we be a little wild together,

Circe asked as we lay in her den of armchairs,
the temptress fluttering behind glasses.
Our foreheads felt the same, possibly we were both ill.
I undressed her, got her into pajamas,
read to her from an orange tome,
the first bound thing my fingers found.

I thought of Shackleton's expedition,
how the Endurance snapped in the pack ice.
How he dead reckoned the ship's boat,
about the size of a canoe—
willed his men through eight hundred miles
of Antarctic waters, stars the closest warmth,
galaxies closer than any landfall.
How the land fell.

Never mind the rain soon stops,
winter passes, spring ends;
we'll sleep like tortoises,
waken and plant vegetables together.

I lay beside her, removed her thick glasses
and we huddled under blankets
while I told her story after story
of lizards, of the evolutionary abyss, the reason
for the width of railway tracks.

I described tropical fish, their frenzied breeding
in large pools in Valletta, St. Sebastian
and the astringency of arrows, natural selection
and survival of the finches.
Sometime in the night, my strategy evolved.

Ulysses Asks His Ex-Wife to Dinner

Dulci, tartuffo, decorum est—but no moody mori here,
I make no nostalgia of this, propose nothing,
niente but the dish itself—still some polls show me well ahead
and others have me lagging the big spenders
relentlessly polite, they imagine themselves good or lucky.

Then here's to the elect, the polished, potted, poutless
primi piatti, sauteed topknot of fiddlehead fern
pot au feu, fire in the kettle still—

And why not be still, as in the stillness of breath held
when the lungs expel then forget what's next—well
into the wild orchid's beginning we know,
we're strung like bells amazed to be *bells* at all,

like the knelling in the Piazza di Spagna
above the small room near the Spanish Steps
where Keats died by the not still fountain,
still fountain enough for my hands
                                        not
yours not
            now, and why would I not

be yours—I will—I *will* translate myself
from the original,
turn as Michelangelo sleeping four to a bed with his masons,
your slip-hipped emissary
of sweet remembrance, best
guardian of the here-to-for, therefore
a fading dragonfly aloft on thinnest air.

No double entendres from me—
neither grace notes nor seductive turn of phrase,
though as for praise,
coscia di monaca—those plums grown plump
in Tuscany—nun's thigh.

I can be that, no?
Even now, for you, my love—what falls freely
from the hand—a spotted apricot, gnarly apple,
the remembered fig.

Circe and Ulysses Go Out For Sushi

For all the world
what looked exactly like gold leaf,
the chef arranged on her sushi.

1) Exercise: write six stanzas without mentioning love.
2) Exercise: write six stanzas without meaning longing.
3) Exercise: write about the quest for the not-yet-seen in an entirely original alphabet, be descriptive and specific. Color is important.
4) Exercise: show how the image of the inherited enemy is already sleeping in the nervous system. Denial is required.

Circe asked whether the gold was edible.
Ulysses would turn himself to gold for her.
The chef put several strands, thin as angels, in her hand.
The gold moved in the current.
She did not know what to do.
The chef closed her hand with his hand around the filaments of gold.
She put the gold in her mouth.
Where it melted and she glistened like a prayer.
The chef looked on, pleased.
Circe, very pleased.

Who here does not have the shape of the predator?

The chef forms a slice of yellowtail and rice into the shape of a pyramid.
It is love he is asking for.

Obdurate blue.
Ulysses wishes for the harbor where the cargo hides.
His body takes an invisible position.
Often waiting.
Dark rivers, absence, pauses, time's fool.

The chef watches Circe as she glistens.
Gold enters the picture.

Turns Out Circe Has Something of a Past

Have I told you about the year I danced?
Before we met, in clubs, I stripped for drunks.
You would think the closeness crushing,
but no one said a word, no one ever touched me.

A lonely art, like painting without models, without light,
and I, a brilliant tease, brushed naked note by note, deepened
to a place with no bar stools, no shy staring.

Sometimes I stripped in clubs behind private walls in old Miami
where I could conjugate my nakedness—
nudo, nudas, nuda, nudamos, nudan. No
narcissism, this wasn't pumping iron. *Nada,*
it was nothing for me to do it all for them.

You ask why I didn't say about the dancing.
One day, a man watched as he spoke into a telephone
smaller than a sparrow.

He took me with him,
talked for five days without stopping
while I ate and slept and danced for him.
He said his insides had annealed,
had alloyed his metals.

Spoke like that, the talker.
Called me his cockatiel, but without the irony—
bird of paradise, the female,
the one without plumage.

Toward the end, I saw my body from above—
no bird—
a fish scooped mottled in the net—
quivering, quiet, glazed.

Ulysses in the "Loon's Watch"

I'd trade whatever I could find for salt cod,
sit on barrels or shipping crates and eat.
There was no trouble passing for one of them
the way I dipped bread into bowls of hot feijoada.
It was there I learned my house is encircled.

You'll want to know the rooms are full of remnants—
on the carpets, on the floors, in the corners.
Don't be afraid to rub your heart against the banister.

O my gentle other self, I leave you my Oxo Good Grips
nonslip cleaning tools, the tilting toilet brush,
my atomic ant vacuum.
A sleek banana stand, all chrome—
perfect for serving seedless grapes as well,
or ripening tomatoes-on-the-vine.

I give you the model on the cover
in Gideon Oberson's print bandini, cropped top
with loop detail, and white wide-leg pants, semi-sheer.
She'll want the raffia tote six years from now,
then make a gift of your own ruefulness.

Take heart, my second self.
There will be backward glances that give you hope.
There will be cheese sellers speaking the ardent tongue of your
childhood.
There will be prehistoric ooze under a weak winter sun.
There will be train tracks stropped bright under streetlights.
There will be primeval forests—with grief, and without.

Meet me in the Loon's Watch, near closing time,
the table by the emergency door, under the red sign.
Wear the baggy trousers the color of old glacier ice—
I'm the one they no longer fit.

Telemachus in San Miguel

My midnight over in which no incense, no scented arms no ankle bells.
Neither hookah nor adagio nor windows shut against the crowbar
slice of moon,
yet windows anyway, courtyard below, its scattering of pulque pots
and Spanish tile in ochre, burnt sienna—
hands sewing something yellow in the lightless morning,
stitching closed night's parted lips with raveled flax.

While close in the creel fresh fish red and scaly,
fish with Indian names,
hua-chi-nan-go, gilled god of the shallow waters—

what use each month below my window fish mongers
send another virgin,
and who am I to put an end to this?

One carries the sea god roasted over the fire pan—
"For you,"—*"usted"*—the formal you,
her hands held high above her head.

As if she knows no better,
better merchants come here as they come,
carting fish and virgins, Madonnas with their red-scaled gods.

They know, and still weave morning in this courtyard
out of ochre tile and greenless vines
below my windows,
skyless dawn above.

Ulysses' Son is Thankful for Discreet Friends

I licked the milk from her coffee spoon,
and you were kind enough not to mention it.
Understand, the milk—pale though creamier than I'm accustomed,
spiced with fresh-cracked coffee beans, vanilla and a touch of lipstick—
sang out with a kind of longing no man could overlook.

But it was just a spoon, a thing, made to satisfy—
silver, smooth and round, and that her hand lingered on the handle
and mine over hers was a small matter of angle and convenience,
like the heart's low inclination in winter, though I admit

this sort of thing could happen to anyone and happened
once before in the South of France, where I saw the jazz man
turn his horn to smoldering coal,
passed it through a field of waving hands, passed it burning
from hand to hand while his drummer worked a double-rhythm
on the bass and bourbon flowed from a copper cup.
Blowing single notes, like the moans of distant sheep,
the sky darkened and the ground dissolved. I swear

nothing more than fondness, then, the night I took her empty beer,
wet and smeared with palms, after she turned in for the night—
and while I held the beaded bottle to my face
for what must have seemed a long, long time, I forget
how her lips had brushed the neck,
her tongue worked the inner rim
or that small shudder when she pressed the cold
against her summer blouse.

Ulysses Mourns the Stolen Figs

Someone was taking them in the night,
the fig trees bared of half their fruit.

I know what you think—
animals, maybe raccoons, or night birds—
but the wild cherries hadn't been touched,
nor the peaches, and the rock walls girding the orchards
haven't looked right for weeks,
crenelated, crumbled.

Armed with tridents and machetes
we took turns as sentinels—
set the walls with torches and borrowed
from a cleric three guard dogs big as ponies.

The dogs patrolled with muzzles in the air,
barking whenever they liked,
what did it matter to them?

We found nothing, no one,
for all the noise and the sharp things in our hands,
but the thirsty dogs uncovered a cistern,
full of water, ancient, clear—
and this treasure in a dry country
convinced the neighbors and tradesmen
that our process is irreversible,
convinced us of a certain modesty in things,

that often as not it's the night wind that bends
the branches low and bears away what fruit it likes,
and all of this—call it a kind of faith—
gave our masons and dowsers, even the Buddhists
in the mountains, to conclude
we are as easily hidden from as seen.

Penelope Remembers the Miracle at Bar Harbor, Maine

"Tide can take a boat half-out to Labrador," one old-timer said,
we there on the jetty, pulled through early morning fog and rain
to wood smoke lifting from the cook shack chimney.

Twenty-two and newly wed, leaking love and money
from New Mexico to Maine until we both were out of both,
but neither of us done with hunger nor the other—

The sky spread gun metal,
yellow rain slickers slid through the cook shack,
men cowled into priests, their thick hands cupping
bowls of steaming something—

Propane stove and iron pot,
fish stew simmering for weeks non stop,
the cook adding and adding—
whatever the lobster men bring in, everything
they bring in, goes in—

one ladled cup after cup, the sacred thing itself—
the coral lobster and the cod, mussels, soft-belly clams,
red bliss potatoes—breakfast.

Did you want me to believe?
The coffee and the rain, onion bread
braided like hawsers, like life lines, the grain living in our fists.
Did you want me to grieve?
Our arms stretched out and out, on them light, the clouds.

Circe Taunts Our Hero About His Monastic Moment

"Mad Mary's Cousin Nick's," Regina's homage to Bohemia.
Another night at the Tattoo Ball, the United Monks
of the Brotherhood of Starslick out in force to assay my body chemistry,
And you, mad Monk, are nowhere near.

The Brothers revere the perky flair of my red caftan,
Cut deep and low, a reverence of the sort reserved for Nefertiti,
Winds of the Nile, darkest blue of pagan dreams—
Tired of sackcloth and piety, these friars.

Smitten by my string of beans, like gilt bibles draped
over one bare shoulder, down along my barer back—

My long legs tattooed with fire breathing dragons,
Black dahlias deck my thighs, entwine my perfect arms.

Each breast a replica of Lady Liberty, do their part to light the world.

Hey fiddle-de-dee, it's the Benedictine life for thee.
Or is this remedial Zen?

Brings to mind the Buddhist Monk, a novitiate
assigned to sweep the path, its worn-smooth stones in autumn.

Fiercest concentration, every vein and bract.
Each time his master found new fault—
Stray twig or new-blown leaf marred the stubborn rocks.

'True, it is nearly right,' he finally told my friend.
And gathering a clutch, spilled a cloud of yellows, reds and browns.

Like swept stones, we women pave your life—

It's tattoos, beans and beasts that cover all we know
Of am and want. Watch.
My heart fixes where your hand still holds the broom.

Ulysses Hums the *Ave Verum*

With the Benedictines
Moose Jaw, Saskatchewan

If you don't know Mozart's *Ave verum corpus*
you are more fortunate than I can say
because your life is yet unruined by its purity.

A motet for four-part choir, strings and organ—
46 slow bars—not a single note too many
nor one note short of heaven.

The only mark is *sotto voce,* our master wanted sound
beneath the voice. Beneath this sky,
neither butte nor mesas rise.

These streets sheltered bootleggers once,
were home to brothels in the Gilded Age.
Now matins call and here am I, trading work
for room and board, no cowl or cassock, but pullover and jeans.

Except for chant, there are no words but words remembered,
no sound but the sound of work,
the split and crack of firewood, percussion of building hammers.

After vespers, evenings in my room belong to me.
I hum *sotto voce* while I think, hum the *Ave verum,*
hum the voices, organ, strings.

Odd, how long it takes to read the silence.
When we chant at night the wolves join in,
we sing the middle of the world to sleep.

What is Taken

I'll take a sherry, Circe starts,
though lately it's been not sherry but a rye—

Take one with me? and I think, why, what better
than to take a drink in early evening
with Circe, though lately it's been not
early evening but waning afternoon.

And if poured of a size she likes we stand
long minutes by a window, one more glass
between the Sound and Great Peconic Bay.

Her ring hand flowing to the cupboard,
she turns her head, and we watch, say, early cardinals,
one burning crimson, one a smoldered dun,

take birdseed from the wheaten light and tilt
a sober look at us, our drinks and crystal,
the held-fast pose. Beyond, our twins drift
above the beach—

notice how they lift their glasses,
how the shadows cover each.

Penelope Draws From Life

I miss the old simplicity of things,
seashore with boardwalk and a book, not reading.
Evenings with Haydn's quartets, singing the viola line to myself.

Maybe I'm obsessive, the Big Moment just a moment,
nothing more, it comes, it goes,
armor shatters, life goes on—

I give an art class in the fall, "Drawing from Life"—
students practice sketching with one eye closed
so their hands invent dimension guided by rhythm only.

I'll pose as their life model while reading pages from my journals
as they work to cover up with charcoal
where my bones cleave to my flesh and my body bends into its sighing.

I spend my nights wondering why Ulysses wouldn't let me watch him die.
He waited until nearly midnight, after even the hospice nurse gave in.
Just before I left, he demanded two teaspoons of tea,
two more of wine and another dose of morphine.

When he could no longer speak, I lifted his transparent hand.
Squeeze mine, I asked, *if you agree to share what you find out,*
and when I felt a finger tighten—

it was right to go.

THREE

Cavatina

It may be there's a time of day when everything
is cool and silent, the day itself cool and silent,
the kitchen lights barely on, or not, say,

a morning, summersoft, the single cypress
swaying in something only it can feel,
the bread in its basket, the linen in its drawer.

Everything put away and the day not even started—
peace like calligraphy, the stars set, just now
lighting fishermen through another world.

It may be such a time exists though I can't find it,
Lord knows, not even in the Cavatina movement
of Beethoven's late quartet.

Should I say that it is short,
it is short and incomparably beautiful?
Would saying so make a difference?

Or should I say that while listening, I'm obsessed
with the spelling of Beaujolais, which I cannot seem
to manage without a dictionary, though

I can remember the taste of each growth,
the graininess, near nobility for such a slight wine,
of a Brouilly from a decent year, or the hint

of raspberries in a good Fleurie.
Or should I say that Beethoven died
before the first performance of this work,

or should I say only that I have not, even so,
given up my obsession with love?
That it is a possible thing—

possible as cistern, possible as caique,
accessible as fountain, as easily plucked
as frankincense, sensate as sea urchins

with their long spines, idling red-tipped
in the shallow tidal pools.
In my obsession, I have the whole piece by heart

so that its layers line my chest until its parts
are overwhelmed and driven out by the perfect Beaujolais
or by the astonishment of sex or by cool

silent incipient love itself. That,
or the obsession with its slenderness so palpable
that I confuse passion for the real thing,

and who is there to tell me which is which
or even which vices are permissible and which not,
what wine to drink, what bread to eat, why

this obsession with knowing that singular possible thing?
That culpable thing. That frail thing. That frail,
findable, culpable almost possible thing with a hint

of raspberries and even a near nobility for such a slight thing,
out there in the back country roads Sundays in early morning,
everything quiet, everything cool, its tail sprinkled with salt.

About that complimentary welcome Margarita or rum punch

your brochure promised on full-color, slick coated paper
so slippery to the finger tips we wondered
what keeps ink from pearling off the pages
like the pink and crimson petals I found this morning
lining our path from bungalow to breakfast—
poinsettias and birds of paradise,
anthurium with that spike of yellow flowers,
the glossy heart-shaped bract—

petals torn from their hollow stems by last night's rain
falling so tin-sweet and warm as we listened
in our bed with the linen canopy, dreamless and light.
We might have been running down wind like pirates
on a painted sloop, just the way the brochure said—

And our son on the stow-away in the sitting room,
content enough with his own bright berth and feather pillow
couldn't know that later,
I will sleep with my hand flat
against his mother's sternum, fourth finger grazing
one plumped nipple, wrist feathering the other, or doubtless
he'd go moody and sullen, and I think, what?
should I feel guilty about this?

But I do, I do—and rise to bless his breathing
in the other room, willing him to stir.
I want to say I touched his hair, his face—
but it was enough to watch—
and so sway to the sounds of bells and flutes,
salt smell of offshore breeze,
until a primeval hint of light
brightened the louvered windows—

By breakfast, the beach was dry and white as pictured
but for those few fallen petals your raker missed.
You can't know how grateful I was for each,
cupping the clearing sky in meager folds.

Surely thinking I did it just for them,
I gave one to my son, one to my wife—
two hearts, extravagant and wet.

Augustine's Early Daffodils

A happy fault, a blessed wound. Blesséd.
So says Augustine in *The Confessions.*

Every work of art contains a seed of death.
Stigmata, tattoos.
I no longer remember who said that, or if it's true.

Well, we never came so close to the breath of the enemy,
as my grandfather used to say.

No doubt it's very rash, to disconnect this way.

I will become instead a decorative drawing
with matting to match the sofa, and yet, I just heard myself
breathe in the primal germ of flowers.

Out back where we used to live,
there was a black oak or pin oak, one of those,
planted below a semi-circle of white and yellow daffodils,
thick despite the maze of roots,

and the daffodils began to sprout through snow
earlier every year. December or January.
By February, surely.

I wanted to push them back down
through the roots, back into the frozen earth
where they'd be safe and warm in their corms.

These daffodils were each a famous beauty
in ancient times, I knew. So.

It was clear at first, but later, snowed again.
The planes bound for LaGuardia diverted
themselves over our rooftop.
Twilight snow, curls of smoke from the chimney
and the neighbors' chimneys, and a United jet,
coursing low as an osprey, its windows open,
passengers tossing handfuls of powdered rice.

We ran out in surprise, of course.
My wife and child laughing and pointing with joy.

Late in the night, some cream and wine
to ring in the ides of March,
and I grabbed an atlas with relief maps
despite the aching in my back,
pointed at mountains many continents away,

on top of each, a temple, I predicted,
the soothsayer in me,
with bowls of lotus blossoms, kimonos,
daggers, six trained falcons,
lacquered boxes filled with star fruit,
cup after cup of Chinese tea.

Votive

Here the bar's a wooden thing, but the ceiling's zinc
and when I tilt back my head I can see how
the philosopher likes his reformed image.

It's the image of the changing note,
zinc reflection being imprecise, still, in bed
with a fountain of pillows my dream is happy.

Maybe I'll have it later, thick with the night's unwashed kisses—
it won't be morning until the cobblestones are wet
and your hair falls in my hands, palms

pressed together in prayer, falls like fallen angels,
votive in their blinding, like voyeurs, fallen where a vagrant
morning greens the needles of monumental firs.

Smoke vanishes through the too low zinc like music
and bilberry swills across the winter boulevard.
Tell me, traveler, how far from la Tour St. Jacques to Spain?

So late we come to love the cracks in ancient walls,
to hire boats in unknown waters, damn the cost.

Flocking

Slinging a pine-hafted pitchfork, I'm clearing
the Arabians' stables of golden dung and straw,
following hoof prints through the kelp-matted sand
past our Nantucket cottage, the roses and salt crannies,
cranberry bogs and breeze of raw bars,
the high skies, sea grape, spume.

An array of shorebirds flock this morning
as though mustered by some avian god.
"Flock," I say, snapping out the verb
like sheets drying on the line.
"Flock" for the flight of teals in tight formation,
all instinct and feathered undertow.

But I sense you're like the others, wanting the hard
cragged edges of words, not soft wet work of dreams,
dreams so symbol-stuffed, cloud shrouded,
full of indifference and iffyness.

So lie a while with your bifocals, morning paper
& espresso while I bear us back a quarter century
to that patterned quilt in Nancy, when your hair
was red, a fetching lacy nothing slipped one shoulder,
and shorebirds flocked our dream sky black and white,
and what else could I do but give you Joyce,
now dyply hypnotised or hopeseys doeper himself
and the shines he cuts, shinar, the screeder,

fouyoufoukou! shriek his shorebirds,
like the ones that flock my dream sky black and white,
like sirens, like French kids with sand-colored flesh,
like cats flocked with mange, fish-eyed cats,
transparent cats that skitter through this port town

I've seduced you deep, deep into with spiny words
and fake Arabian horses, quaint hoof prints, golden dung
and pissyellow straw, my dirty hands pulling you
Through winding streets and rutted alleys,
pitchfork sharp into the hollow.

Metals

For months, dialogue followed us like love-starved dogs.
The candlelit restaurant in Firenze where we first met
ravioli with butter and sage. The leather smell
of shoe stores mixed with the first bite of autumn air,
someone smoking a sack of olives in their chimney.

To arrive, we've taken our own good time—
calling at the missions, lost in unknown waters,
driven by a storm, boots and uniforms soaked,
rifles waterlogged, we arrived at an island inhabited by rats
as big as boys, with long tails, and bags over their abdomens.

They were friendly, holding out their little hands
to beg for food, tugging at our white ducks,
but in the end they proved expert thieves,
even lifting hardtack from our knapsacks.

When the third wave landed at Normandy,
one soldier, known for his amorous excess,
found a helmet in which a pair of doves had nested.
No one could let go of such a thing.
Who would not wish to die for a hieroglyph?

The dove's wings covered with silver reads the Psalm,
and her feathers were yellow gold.
Or, let's suppose it's not metals after all,
but tools that ferry us from life to life.

What I mean to say, the dove's an important sign—
the golden medulla, the philosopher's stone—
a helmet filled with something we'll never have.

The Turning

It’s not been cold this winter. But tonight—
the ground is hard and grassless, rhododendron leaves
warp tight against the chill,
the sky is clear and piped with stars.

There’s the smell of wood smoke and something faintly arctic—
an Inuit's fire—two brown-toothed Eskimos
and their crescent-lidded boys stropping whale bone knives
while drying seal skins by the light.

Later, mom and dad turn beneath the quilt,
hold quiet while close by their children sleep,
their faces and hands rough, bodies soft as seal skin,
slippery as otters.

Outside, twenty sled dogs huddle, ears cocked
to the faint chop of a single-engine Piper Cub flying
low and toward the moon.

Under the bare cherry trees something still
and ageless seeps up into the bones—
frozen earth, echo of near firesides,
slow breathing of the season.

Chiaroscuro

Two of the oddest ducks bobbing white
above and below a thin band of black
and blacker black from blunted beak
to necklace spun from snow
were nowhere in my tattered field guide.

Tourists then, south for the winter from Quebec,
or far as Baffin Bay, because the white was arctic,
brilliant and blazing, and the black the whole volume
of polar sky where it soars rounded and majestic as the Duomo,

where I once stood satisfied as Filippo Brunelleschi,
another rarity in a watery world,
his genius fixed and pockets stuffed with coins
stamped with the likeness of some Medici or local bird?

Someone knows, but it doesn't matter to the ducks
that fly here autumns from a place so sunless
their blacks and whites begin as dun.

Swimming just offshore they utter
desultory kwabs in balanced antiphons,
two strophes each like soloists with laryngitis.

But any language so squat and watermarked
must become another way of seeing—
the way Brunelleschi looked at his cathedral
before leaving for the tavern where no one knew him,
where nothing ever changed,

unlike that first spring day
ice opens in the bay and water becomes water again—
starts to sigh as it parts from itself—

long after the ducks have caught the thrall
of something they can't live without, having slapped
the water twice with mottled wings and flown.

Sainkho and the Trance of Seven Colors

Sainkho, Mongolian throat singer,
both feminine and masculine with her seven-octave range,
piercing highs to guttural lows, is summoned to Morocco
where her vocals, mouth harp and shaman's drum
beckon trance-immersed shamans, invoke forgiveness.

Harmonizing two or more tones at once, faster,
the audience sways back and back—
men move out into the courtyard
as women respond to *rihs,* their songs.

In this healing night of music and trance dancing,
you hear the melody of Aisha Qandisha, female genie,
jinniya of great significance, a beautiful enchantress
with camels' feet. Djivan, the duduk player says,

Aisha controls the men, climbs from the watery world
beneath the floor. Yes, it is bad luck to mention her name,
she must be appeased.

The music waves a sweep of heat through the courtyard,
and the women, too, leave their room and dance,
calling out names of saints, their colors:
Lala Mira, yellow, Lalla Mimuma, pink,
Sidi Hammu, brown, Sidi Musa, blue.

The frenzy builds, entranced dancers collapse,
one after another. Maioli, percussion, conch, says,
I am not going to tell you that a woman falls
because of devils or something like that!

We have never seen a devil. I have been doing this forever
and I have never seen a devil. But she feels the emotion,
the pain in her heart. Sometimes she is blinded or rendered deaf
or mute, afflicted with aching bones, tingling in the knees,
the wrists, dissociation and a doublement de conscience.

And if the song is meaningful and sweet,
she goes into a trance.
There's something inside, in the blood, that leaves you.

The sponsor sends small presents to each musician
For Sainkho, nomad, pilgrim, one conical dish brimming with awe,
one more piled with dates and silver coins.

Torpedo Fuel

She sailed back and forth beneath the Bering Strait,
hunting enemy profiles. Finding one, she'd ping it
with sonar, or get pinged.

In truth, it was a kind of love making for both sides,
an appreciation of surfaces, and always some captain shouting,
"another wave," his eyes closed.
But the enemy fragmented and withdrew into herself,
and so fewer to seduce.
More the loneliness of mariners, then,
the sea's synonymous curve.

The men needed the right music, I knew—
brooding, not self-indulgent—
no swelling strings, no crushing weight of cellos
or harmonica cliché, dry, wistful, everyday.

It took a hundred tries to find the sound I wanted—
drove the producer to despair. Ah, but to evoke the cry
of sonar, the high persistent pitch of quest and hope—
and a kind of emptiness, too, spare, devoid of overtones,
something cold and Bergmanesque,
always the actors more gentle, less sure than we credit.

The director, an austere woman who knew most of Sartre
by heart, and quite a lot of Simone Weil,
was patient with me.

When I found the perfect consort,
I invented a kind of jazzy yet soulful sound
by forming wide-spaced seventh and ninth chords
in minor keys, and added a slow samba sort of thing
with tabors beneath, the steady thrum of omens,
open resonance of a bone-like structure,
yet not a bit dissonant.

In one scene, *L'Apparition* berths in Reykjavik
just as an American lingerie maker
shoots his fall catalogue on the airport tarmac,
the models equidistant and diaphanous,
mouths medieval with a rumor of departure.

So this mariner comes on to a brunette
from Venice, CA in a bar by slicing top
and bottom from a fresh baguette
and pouring a rust-colored liquid through and through
into a shot glass until it runs clear.

Drinking it down, he hallucinates in French—
and she falls for it, interrogating his disorder.
Of course, he only tells her it's torpedo fuel—
he's beautiful as she—and this is Iceland.

They cut the scene,
but it inspired the main love theme.
The pit orchestra played boldly when they handed me the prize.
How those chords melded fantasy and verité!
Haunting, if I may say so, and maybe a touch of hesitation.

Ferdinand Victor Eugène Delacroix Conducts His Interview

The last visitor of the night,
born a Scots' laird, now third mate, stork-thin—
a gut, a bone, a tooth—
the painter's jug of jade wine
meant to calm him, though the rain
had turned to snow on deck, and back
to rain, and this the fifth watch,
they paced together, circled,
shoulder to epaulet, a sea apart.

The mate wanted to tell Delacroix
about pear blossoms, white, blanch, blank,
stunning white as a thousand moths,
and the deep green willows,
a blizzard of springs flown by
like a mare's mane, fallen
like goose feathers, all night and past,
they hummed *Mother of the World*
by the cold lamps,
their eyes awash and blurred.

He wanted to say something about wilderness,
this laird—the hard infertile soil, exposed rock,
even as the drums pounded from the bow
as the water stiffened in the morning wind,
he wanted to pin something down,
one thing down—
the name of a star, a burst of light,
the odor of jungle off Sudan,
the way a certain fruit glows on the tree
in its own soft nimbus,
the moss covered mouths of caves.

From the remains of his pocket
the laird produced an ostrich-feather-fan,
soft inner feathers of the bird
bound by a thin length of string.

For you, he said to Delacroix,
and as they couldn't find
a single farewell song between them,
they took the short way back.

Anatomy of Coral

Medications alter, but her topography
shifts and sways to stay intact.

I play Mozart, let her linger
over eternally returning rondos.
That slow movement the masseuse times
with oils, circles, aromatics.

No one can cover her feet,
she needs to see her toes.

Moving to the big island of Kapa,
we watch the wide reef lashed by waves
on the channel, a man wrestling with a net,
massed fish plunge twice a day into a dinghy.

He offers buckets, fat sardines
I grill over penga wood on the lanai,
while a lone humpback whale breeches
in shallow water, nearly silent, the same time every day.

Waiting.

We have extra food, a stove, two cots,
an oil lamp that smokes blue black,
a tiny rubber boat, some books, some weeks.

A constant thudding, neither waves nor falling coconuts.

Parrot fish, brilliant yellow and blue,
glitter the coral ledge
and crown-of-thorns starfish, nibble and dart.

Two waves become a pair of sharks,
spotted fins, epaulets, mottled and elegant,
playing in the water.

I bring her plates of cypress-polyps, pink minnows dotted
with olive, grazed ashen cauliflowers sprayed
with scarlet, striped tubers of blackened copper,
a porous, saffron liver of a great animal, that,
or artificial fire of mercury,

wisps of thorns dripping sanguine
and chaliced mother of pearl, like an urn, covered
with coralline cartilage that has assumed
the shapes of flowers and garden fruits—
the terrestrial humors of coral body.

A doctor's flown in from the mainland
with machines to count the finite brittles.

We burden him with space, reduction, dialogue, venom,
a strict accounting of fever—
counting backward toward the flood,

and for the return trip,
his sack looted of its melancholy,
its paper nautilus, the chambered conch.

I Had As Lief Embrace the Porter

1.

I meant to spirit back my son,
come to terms on gestures under the brittle crust of daylight
    as if nights dredged up from another epoch
had siphoned off the whole, thick, nerve numbing
    blackness and lifted away
the ineffable noon, no sooner done than there he was
at Naples writing letters home—
or on his side, reclining on his hip—
not thinking how once his old man's bones were quick as foxes on the hill
but slowed, sinking downward under massive clouds—

How is it my son had after all
    as lief embrace the porter at his hotel,
as give out his "loosen up, Dad," leaving me tips
and the smallest kisses for my trouble,
salving the ache where I failed him once again—
    what to do but honor him with coffee and figs in a sunny chair?
Though he says, pears only, and for once, Dad,
no bounty to the prayerless dead, ok?

2.

But light is what he wants from me—
we know this though he won't say—
then understand at once, the open sky has answers
and a certain bold assurance so I say,

    let's rent one of those metal boats, bring the kosher dogs,
    beer, charcoal, burn the things to crisps
and under double white clouds we're off aboard the skiff—
we have my coffee cup,

we have rainwater washing out the scuppers,
we have quiet—
so quiet now you can hear the land crabs pacing
back and forth across the dock—

3.

There's the drama, out where you're shunted
past the uncommon shelter of common life,
arm over shoulder and shoulder under arm—
I'd just like to take this opportunity to warn
the remaining pretenders of the earth,
the whole earth in its simplicity and instinct
in all such elusive ambitions:
"It is not enough to cover the rock with leaves."

Instead we visit this small planetarium for kids,
though the room dredges up its own silt mode
as the docent points to the Milky Way
with his phosphorescent lash of light—
our galaxy, he says, and says how big it is
and says how little of it we occupy,
our middling, evanescent, love soaked speck of solar system,
there in that tiny swirl at the outmost edge of another swirl
only slightly larger than our moon-numbed own.

4.

Meanwhile, down here in our local zip code of a spiral
ashes with the taste of ash navigate through space,
and with their winged machines drop through the open skylight—
            odor of sweating wood still on the hearth,
dew-wet flowers—devastation along the promenades—
mist of canals over the fields, the ropes stretched
steeple to steeple and let's, I say, go home,
            put on the good china, silver, linen—
spread the morning paper on the carpet.

Come on back to me from Naples, son, or, better,
I pack my make-do luggage, suppose—
            oh me, my irrepressible heart
            and what it thinks it wants:
my boy in jeans half-way to hay,
before the credences of summer set their teeth.

Morning in Morelia, Blurred and Still

As they toll at five a.m., the church bells of Morelia sound
as sound itself might chase the drought—
and then morning, blurred and still,
the air heavy with stubbornness and unspent rain.
There, the cobalt blur of hummingbird,
and there, wagon ruts and the fossil heart,
a thousand years of broken promises and crying dogs.

I'm alone, and not—
up soon enough to touch the chill still moored
to the each bell's iron tongue and stippled
to pipes and petals in the garden.
Up soon enough to feel the flanks of plaster holding
plank by plank what frames the house,
once a monastery, they say, they say it
in a language earlier than Cortez.

So let the church bells bless the sheaves of herbs
with Aztec names, the chilies drying above the stove
in braided strands, each braid, each herb the devotion
of a slower angel, it's spirit caught and kept for luck—
and I, willing captive, raveling solitude one thread at a time,
searching everywhere for another pod of witchcraft,
hefting samples in my palm, upending stones,
fumbling among the pulque pots and southern stars.

An hour before matins, a young priest yawns and fills
his chalice in the darkened nave—
But I choose the slower path to what I worship,
stubborn, foolish, failing man—the church bells
tell I'm less than what I used to be.

A half-century of believing exchanged, useless coin,
for what's worth knowing here—
how to scoop the pulp from avocado, spoon
the coffee, arrange the single lily in the vase.

Let the bells bless the wooden angels
and the abuelita who carves them in the plaza,
may the bells preserve the ancient stones beside the lake,
may they guide the small girl who carries the earthen bowl—
its mound of morning light—weightless, yet enough
to flood and flood the room.

Jeffrey Levine has won the Larry Levis Prize from *The Missouri Review*, the James Hearst Award from *North American Review*, *The Missouri Review Poetry Prize*, and *The Kestrel Poetry Prize*. His poems have appeared in *Antioch Review*, *Barrow Street*, *Beloit Poetry Review*, *Ploughshares*, *Poetry International*, *Quarterly West*, and elsewhere. He is Editor-in-Chief of Tupelo Press, an independent literary press located in Dorset, VT.

The author would like to thank: *The Missouri Review*, *The North American Review*, *Kestrel*, the Skylands Artists and Writers Association and the Great River Arts Institute, as much for their generosity as for the encouragement and sustenance their awards and fellowships provided. Special thanks for the support and generous criticism of other poets, especially Nancy Naomi Carlson, Mary Stewart Hammond, Janet Holmes, Roy Jacobstein, Thomas Lux, and Dianne Williams Stepp. Most of all, abundant gratitude for the love and understanding of my family.

Pavement Saw Press, Box 6291, Columbus OH, 43206
All prices include postage. Order direct from the publisher.

Dana Curtis, ***The Body's Response to Famine***
Transcontinental Award Winner. Poems from *Colorado Review; Columbia Poetry Review; Denver Quarterly; Hayden's Ferry Review; Nimrod; Volt; West Branch* and others.
"If her book were a garden, it would be a place of black ice and live water"
– Rikki Ducornet 80 pages, $60 hc, $12 pb

Gordon Massman, ***The Numbers***
"The Numbers, is a hydra-headed, incantatory howl honoring the appetite that gorges on spillage from the riptides of desire and its near-spiritual flesh-fruits."
– Jack Myers 96 pages, 8" x 9," $75 hc, $12 pb

Hands Collected: The Books of Simon Perchik (1949-1999)
Includes 59 new poems and complete editions of every book. This is Perchik's seventeenth collection of poetry. 612 pages, 6" x 9," $100 hc, $30 pb

Carl Thayler, ***Shake Hands***
A series of poems about friends and his first perfect bound full length collection since the early seventies. People from Tom Clark to Mark Wallace are endorsing it. 64 pages, $10

Ivan Argüelles & John M. Bennett, ***Chac Prostibulario***
A poem written in 7 languages, to impress your unlingual compadres, there is nothing like it. 92 pages, 8" x 9," $10

Tod Thilleman & Bill Jensen, ***Entellechy***
A wide-sized art book, good for coffeetables, coffeehouses, museums, your house, bathhouse, whatever. If you dislike poetry, this has fewer poems than most poetry books; if you like poems, these are ovidean dense and cartesian deep. 64 pages, 8" x 9," $10

Errol Miller, ***Magnolia Hall***
Miller is one of the finest southern experimental writers in the US. His unique use of the known to form a new geography resonates with perception.
72 pages, 6" x 9," $8

Will Alexander, ***Above the Human Nerve Domain***
Oreshas, angels, and tigers perforate these pages. This poetic descendant of Rilke and Lamantia lays out an adroit cosmology.
72 Pages, 6" x 9," $75 hc, $12 pb

Richard Blevins, ***Fogbow Bridge: Selected Poems***
"An exemplum of method and music at once, and how they serve to keep intelligence on track, flourish a clean wit we can do with these days." – Robert Kelly
128 pgs, 6" x 9," $60 hc, $12 pb